WHAT'S YOURS

KEZIAH WARNER

CURRENCY PRESS
The performing arts publisher

Red Stitch THE ACTORS' THEATRE

CURRENT THEATRE SERIES

First published in 2025
by Currency Press Pty Ltd,
Gadigal Land, Suite 310, 46–56 Kippax Street, Surry Hills, NSW 2010, Australia
enquiries@currency.com.au
www.currency.com.au

in association with Red Stitch

Typeset by Brighton Gray for Currency Press.
Cover image shows Carissa Lee, Christina O'Neill and Kevin Hofbauer.
Cover design by Mathias Johansson for Currency Press.

Currency Press acknowledges the Traditional Owners of the Country on which we live and work. We pay our respects to all Aboriginal and Torres Strait Islander Elders, past and present.

NATIONAL LIBRARY OF AUSTRALIA

A catalogue record for this book is available from the National Library of Australia

Contents

What's Yours was first performed at Red Stitch Actors' Theatre, Euro-Yroke, Boon Wurrung Country, St Kilda, Melbourne, on 26 July 2025, with the following cast and creatives:

JO	Christina O'Neill
SIMON	Kevin Hofbauer
LIA	Carissa Lee

Director, Isabella Vadiveloo
Set and Costume Designer, Bianca Pardo
Lighting Designer, Rachel Lee
Composition & Sound Design, Grace Ferguson and Ethan Hunter
Stage Manager, Jessica Smart
Assistant Stage Manager, Ella Thompson
Hansen Graduate Assistant Director, Roisin Wallace Nash
Hansen Graduate Attachement, Sookyung Shin

CHARACTERS

JO
SIMON
LIA

Early twenties, then late thirties, then early forties.

A NOTE ON MISOGYNY (internalised and otherwise):

Lia isn't pathetic, don't play her that way.
Jo isn't cold, don't play her that way.

FORMAT

Words in (brackets) are unspoken.

Speech rhythm is largely dictated by line breaks.

A line break without punctuation mid-speech is a microbeat.

A speech indicated without dialogue is a character not knowing what to say.

/ is an overlap.

— is a cut-off.

This playtext went to press before the end of rehearsals and may differ from the play as performed.

1

This scene might be played not as an exact recreation of the past, but as a memory.

Eighteen years ago. A hallway. The sounds of a house party through the wall.

LIA *and* JO *alone, maybe leaning against the wall. They're drunk. Silence for a moment.*

LIA: This is nice.
    Just us.
JO: I can ask them all to leave.
LIA: You can't.
    Can you?
JO: It's your party.
LIA: They're very noisy.
JO: You have a lot of friends.
LIA: I don't know half of them.
JO: Everyone likes you.
LIA: I'm very likeable.
JO: It's annoying.
LIA: You're annoying.
JO: You're like … a nice person.
LIA: And you're awful.
JO: I know. I'm mean.
LIA: Nah, you're alright.
JO: You want another drink? I'll get it for you.
LIA: Yes! Don't leave!
JO: We should dance again.
LIA: Still is good.
JO: I got us sausage rolls, for after.
LIA: Oh my godddd.
JO: I'll heat them up.
LIA: The besttttt.
JO: Barbeque sauce too, even though it's morally wrong.
LIA: Tomato fascist.
JO: Purist.

LIA: I love this hallway.

JO: Same.

LIA: I love living here.

JO: Thanks for having a birthday.

LIA: Did it for you.

JO: Twenty-one!

LIA: I'm so old.

> *Beat.*

JO: I have to ask you something.

LIA: Okay.

JO: It's important.

LIA: … Noooo.

JO: What?

LIA: I'm not doing one of your either-ors.

JO: It's not that.

LIA: Yes it is.

JO: It's not, I swear.

LIA: I know you.

JO: No it's not, this is actually real, this is serious.

LIA: If it's …

JO: It's not!

LIA: Okay …

JO: It's hard to …

LIA: … What? What is it?

> *A loaded beat.*

JO: … Spiders for a face or snake for a penis?

LIA: I hate you.

JO: It's difficult, I know.

LIA: …

JO: Come on. Come onnnnnn. Answer answer / answer answer answer

LIA: Okay okay fine. Fine! Wait let me … Spiders, multiple?

JO: Many, yes.

LIA: Snake.

JO: Really?

LIA: [*thinking she's beaten the game*] I don't have a / penis so it wouldn't even

JO: No, it's not you! No no no. It's not you. It's everyone you ever meet.

LIA: Oh.

JO: Yeah.

LIA: Everyone?

JO: Yes!

LIA: … Still snake.

JO: That's a psychotic answer.

LIA: You'd go spider faces?

JO: Definitely.

LIA: I love faces.

JO: They're not useful.

LIA: Useful?! I couldn't lose faces.

JO: That's just vanity.

LIA: How would you know what people are thinking?

JO: They'd still have eyes!

LIA: You're nuts.

> LIA *closes her eyes.*

JO: I never said they wouldn't have eyes.

LIA: I despise this game.

JO: No you don't. Uh-oh.

LIA: What?

JO: You're sleeping.

LIA: No I'm not.

JO: How many fingers am I holding up?

> JO *doesn't hold up any fingers and* LIA *doesn't open her eyes.*

LIA: Twelve?

JO: You need a secret vom.

> LIA *opens her eyes.*

LIA: Shit. You're so smart.

JO: Want me to come with you?

LIA: Then it wouldn't be secret.

> LIA *exits.*

> SIMON *enters. It's a moment before* JO *sees him.*

SIMON: I hoped you'd be here.

A beat while she takes him in.

JO: You're in luck then.

SIMON: I've seen you, in lectures.

JO: …

SIMON: Creative writing.

JO: I haven't seen you.

SIMON: I'm Simon.

JO: How do you know Lia?

SIMON: Who's Lia?

JO: My housemate.

SIMON: Is she on the course?

JO: This is her birthday party.

SIMON: Oh.

JO: She's in there. Throwing up.

SIMON: Can I get you a drink?

JO: Why?

SIMON: … All the usual reasons … ?

JO: I'm quite drunk already.

SIMON: So am I. Been working up the courage.

JO: What are you being brave for, Simon?

SIMON: Talking to you.

Jo.

JO: Didn't tell you my name.

SIMON: We actually have a tutorial together. You practically run it.

JO: What else do you know?

SIMON: You wrote that short story, about your mother.

JO: A mother. It was 'a' mother. In the abstract. Not my mother.
Something else.

SIMON *grasps for anything to say.*

SIMON: …

… Your house has good ceilings.

Beat. JO *looks up.*

JO: I hope I always live here.

SIMON: I'll buy it for you.

JO: I'll give you the ceilings.

SIMON: I'll give you the shirt off my back.

JO: I'll give you my kidney.

SIMON: My lungs.

JO: Let's get married.

SIMON: Let's have kids.

The smallest, almost imperceptible beat.

JO: I lied to you before.

SIMON: We mustn't lie to each other.

JO: I have seen you. You sit at the front, in lectures.

SIMON: I'm very attentive.

JO: I like your face, Simon.

SIMON: I like your face, Jo.

JO: I'd like to lick your ears.

SIMON: I'd like to eat your elbow.

JO: I'd like to take your face and give you my face.

SIMON: I'd like that.

JO: Do you want to kiss me?

SIMON: Yeah.

JO: Go on then.

SIMON *moves towards* JO *as* LIA *re-enters.*

LIA: Actually.

Would you hold my hair?

JO: Of course.

LIA: Who are you?

SIMON: I'm Simon.

JO: Come on, we've got to dance after this.

LIA: Promise me!

JO: I promise.

LIA: Who was that?

JO *looks lingeringly at* SIMON.

JO: … No-one.

2

The present day.

LIA *and* SIMON *'s.* LIA *is lost in thought.* SIMON *is chopping vegetables. He has been talking, perhaps for some time.*

SIMON: Which would take a lot of pressure off, at least for the next semester.

It's the same class so I wouldn't need to do all the prep again.

But obviously with most of the book advance going on the treatments, not that I'm …

Not that I'm (complaining). I'm really happy about that, obviously.

But I'll talk to them to see if there's a longer contract that could be

Just so we know, I know, where I stand and

Lia?

LIA: Sorry. Yes?

SIMON: You okay?

LIA: Fine.

Smells good.

SIMON: I haven't started cooking it.

LIA: I'm hungry.

SIMON: I was just saying it's a relief, teaching next semester.

LIA: Absolutely. Yeah, that's great. I'm proud of you.

SIMON: Sure you're okay?

LIA: Perfect.

SIMON: Would you like some wine?

LIA: I shouldn't.

SIMON: You can have a night off.

LIA: I know it's boring.

SIMON: It's not.

LIA: No. It is, it's … [*Genuinely realising*] It's so fucking boring.

SIMON: I didn't say that. I don't think that.

LIA: No, let's have some wine.

SIMON: Really?

She gets up, gets wine and glasses.

LIA: Yeah! Let's get drunk. Let's have fun. You look really good at a chopping board. You could be on TV.

SIMON: What are you doing?

LIA: Seducing you. Put the knife down.

He does. She puts her arms round his neck, kisses him.

[*Like it's sexy*] I'm not even ovulating.

SIMON: [*laughing*] You're wild.

They kiss. She pulls away to pour the wine, fills the glasses very full.

LIA: I'm so wild. Let's have sex. Just about us, all form no function. No endgame, just … Fuck it. Let's do anal.

SIMON *laughs.*

SIMON: Okay.

If you tell me what you're thinking about.

LIA: It's nothing.

SIMON: It's something. I'm never wrong.

LIA: But if I tell you, you won't want to have sex with me.

SIMON: Never.

LIA: Okay but don't say I didn't warn you.

I was thinking about Jo.

Her name drops through the air like a brick.

SIMON: Fuck.

LIA: What you said about her. That thing you

Found out.

SIMON: I shouldn't have told you. I thought it was, I don't know, weird coincidence or something but … I shouldn't have brought up all that … / bad blood.

LIA: No, I'm glad you did.

I think you should do it.

SIMON: Do what?

LIA: Ask her. I think you should ask her.

SIMON: God. I was joking.

LIA: I'm not.

SIMON: I couldn't. I wouldn't even know how to approach …

LIA: Just suggest a catch up. That's not strange, you were together for like six years.

SIMON: Eight.

LIA: Exactly.

SIMON: Must have been ten since I've seen her.

LIA: You saw her at her mum's funeral.

SIMON: Yeah. True, but that was hardly an

 Auspicious

LIA: You said you had a nice talk.

SIMON: / A talk anyway.

LIA: So. It hasn't been that long. A few years?

 We were trying then. Weren't we? Did you tell her?

SIMON: [*he definitely didn't*] I don't know.

LIA: I think she'll say yes. If you ask.

SIMON: Why me?

LIA: She doesn't hate you.

3

A restaurant.

JO: Sorry it took so long to find a time.

SIMON: Drag out the suspense.

JO: Just … busy.

SIMON: Right.

JO: You seem uncomfortable.

 Is your chair … ?

SIMON: It's not the chair.

JO: Can't remember the last time I made someone nervous.

SIMON: I'm not nervous, I'm

 You look great.

JO: Oh. Okay.

SIMON: What?

JO: No. I didn't know we were. Complimenting. You look … good, too

SIMON: Thanks, so do you.

JO: Mm.

SIMON: Sorry. Sorry. How are you?

JO: I'm fine. I'm okay. How are you?

SIMON: Yes, I'm great. You?

JO: I'm fine, Simon.

SIMON: Right. Right.

JO: How's work?

SIMON: Good. You?

JO: Great. You're busy?

SIMON: Yeah, are you?

JO: … Always.

SIMON: Good.

JO: How's your mum?

SIMON: Fine, yours? / Oh!

JO: You know.

SIMON: No, / fuck.

JO: Still dead, / so.

SIMON: Yes, I know, sorry.

JO: You came to the funeral.

SIMON: I did, I know. I'm sorry.

JO: I did call you, after.

SIMON: Yeah, I should have—

You haven't touched your wine.

JO: I'm okay.

SIMON: We can get something else. / I can—

JO: I'm not drinking.

SIMON: What, are you pregnant?

JO: … What?

SIMON: No, sorry. Sorry.

Beat.

So, work. You're still at … ?

JO: Yeah.

SIMON: Wow that must be …

JO: Eleven years. Twelve, nearly.

SIMON: Commitment.

JO: They keep promoting me.

SIMON: I liked that one for window cleaner. With the girl, blowing bubbles that turn / into

JO: Balloons, yeah. How did you know I … ?

SIMON: You have a very distinctive … You have a voice.

JO: [*genuinely*] Thank you.

We got a lot of flack for that, actually. Shouldn't release balloons. Bad for ducks or something.

SIMON: They were imaginary, weren't they?

JO: How's Lia?

SIMON: … She's good.

JO: She didn't want to (join us)?

SIMON: Ah, no she's … work. Workaholic. She's working at the uni now, the lab there, supervises other people's PhDs, can you believe that?

JO: Youngest genius ever. Does she know? That you're meeting me?

SIMON: Of course.

JO: You're acting like you're about to get caught.

SIMON: No I'm not. Caught doing what?

JO: You tell me.

SIMON: No, she's great. She knows. We're great. We're really happy.

JO: …

SIMON: I heard you and that guy got together. From work.

JO: … Connor. Yeah. How'd you hear that?

SIMON: I dunno, the internet?

JO: We broke up. Few weeks ago.

SIMON: Right. I'm sorry.

JO: I read your novel.

SIMON: Did you? Thank you.

Did you like it?

JO: It won awards.

SIMON: Yes but—

JO: So you don't need my opinion.

SIMON: I want it.

JO: Well, it's hard to say.

SIMON: Why?

JO: It was about me.

SIMON: No …

JO: Us. The break-up.

SIMON: No. No-one thinks that.

JO: Well no, because you're a man, aren't you?

SIMON: … What?

JO: People assume you have an imagination. You don't just take exact moments from your own life and put them down on paper like women do, you can make things up. Properly.

SIMON: God, you sound like …

JO: Lia?

SIMON: … People use their lives, as inspiration. You do—did.

JO: I'm not a writer.

SIMON: First thing of yours I read. That story, about your mum.

JO: People don't buy my books.

SIMON: I bought that window cleaner.

    Beat.

I'm writing a new one. It's not going well.

JO: Ah. So this is research.

SIMON: No.

JO: You need new material.

SIMON: Not drinking. What is that? A health thing?

JO: It's not a thing.

SIMON: We should all drink less, probably, shouldn't we.

JO: I just thought: you and me and alcohol, not such an ideal combination. Historically.

SIMON: No. Right. We're um … We're … Me and Lia, we're we're / we're …

JO: Spit it out.

SIMON: We're old, aren't we?

JO: … No. Yes. Old for what?

SIMON: Nearly forty.

JO: Old for clubbing, yes. Old for retirement, no. Young for retirement actually. Young for death. Young for second home ownership, though I've been thinking about it, nice place on the coast / maybe.

SIMON: Old for having kids.

JO: Right.

SIMON: Everyone's already done it, haven't they?

JO: So you and Lia are …

SIMON: No. Yes, but. That's not—

JO: You know you don't have to tell me, don't you? It's not like an STI, you don't have to alert everyone you've ever slept with that you've decided to start spunking in a more constructive context. Is that why she's not here? Is she about to pop?

SIMON: No, she's—We're not. She's not pregnant.

JO: Okay. So what—

SIMON: I saw Connor.

> *Beat. This is a real shock for* JO.

JO: What?

SIMON: In a bar. Like a month ago. He was really drunk. He recognised me. He said you'd just broken up. He said it was because you didn't want children and he did.

JO: Okay.

SIMON: Is that true?

JO: What are you doing?

SIMON: And he said something else.

> I think he thought I'd want to empathise, you know, bitch about you or something.

JO: …

SIMON: I didn't.

JO: I don't care if you did.

SIMON: He said he was blindsided about the whole not-wanting-children thing / because you—

JO: No he fucking wasn't, I was always so clear about—how dare / he fucking—

SIMON: / Because—

JO: Why is he even talking to you about this?

SIMON: Because you …

JO: What?

SIMON: You froze your eggs.

> *Beat.*

JO: Wow. Okay.

SIMON: Before you and him were together he said that you'd told him that you …

> And I was surprised, I mean, shocked because you don't want children, / do you?

JO: Jesus, why would he tell you that?

SIMON: I don't know. But he did. He / did tell me.

JO: I don't want to talk / about this.

SIMON: So have you changed your mind? About / children?

JO: It's none of your business.

SIMON: No I know. I know it's not. I don't have any right to ask. It's up to you, it's your business and your life and your body but I am, I am asking. So please can you just answer. Do you want children? Ever, do you think you might ever, want that. Can you please just answer, yes or no, please.

JO: … No.

SIMON: No, you won't answer / or—

JO: No I don't want children. No. Not ever. / What is this?

SIMON: Right, that's what I thought.
    That's good that's what we
    Because we've been
    Trying
    Me and Lia
    For years actually and it's
    You know, all the terminology is really offensive and
    Geriatric pregnancy and
    You know Lia's got the
    The polycystic ovary stuff and so
    It's not
    It's just … not (happening)
    And we wondered
    We're kind of desperate
    And

JO: I'm going to leave now, Simon.

SIMON: We'd like one of your eggs.
    Or
    All of them.
    We'd like you to give us all of your eggs.
    Please.

    A long pause.

  Say something.

I didn't want to ask you straight away. Really. I wanted us to talk, to catch up. But you not drinking, that threw me and just seeing you is, a lot actually. But I wanted. I did want to wait. Till dessert or.

JO: Dessert?

SIMON: At least.

JO: I don't think pavlova is going to make this better.

SIMON: I know, look / Jo I really—

JO: Not enough meringue / in the world—

SIMON: Pavlova? When did you last go to a restaurant, 1985?

JO: Fuck off.

SIMON: No, sorry I

We'd like you to come for dinner.

JO: We're at dinner now.

SIMON: To us. Come to the house. Talk about it properly.

JO: So you think this is some really elegant solution, do you? Lia with the bad eggs, but here's one I shagged earlier.

SIMON: It's not like that at all.

She gets up to go.

Please, just hear me out.

JO: Fuck. Off.

SIMON: No, sure, okay, that's fair. It's just.

Jo.

You're our last chance.

Beat. She turns back.

JO: If Lia wants a favour, she can fucking ask me herself.

4

LIA *and* SIMON's.

LIA: The first round there were … five?

She looks to SIMON.

SIMON: Six then / five.

LIA: Yes, six eggs were viable but no embryos. Second round five eggs and one embryo, which was implanted but …

SIMON: Didn't … um …

LIA: Third round no eggs were viable.

SIMON: And the advice was that with uh …

LIA: Me being old as fuck.

SIMON: It wasn't worth—

He realises what LIA *has said*

No—

LIA: And that was all we could afford, anyway. The money is just …

SIMON: We had some insurance but not enough and we did get a part rebate on some, but not other and there are all these extra costs and …

LIA: We'd borrowed money, already. From Simon's parents and.

We looked into adoption. But my job is dependent on annual funding now and Simon is freelance so, we look pretty bad on paper. And we still want to explore all the options for the actual, you know, the biological, route, first. But we need.

It's me. You know, they think my uterus is probably … fine. But it's my eggs that are just. Well, I'm the problem. So.

SIMON: Don't / say that.

LIA: It's just the truth.

SIMON: This isn't anyone's fault, I / would never—

LIA: I know. I know. I'm just explaining the … situation.

Beat.

JO: You're so different.

LIA: Okay …

Look, it's complicated. But it's also quite simple. You have something that we want—need. And you can

Set the terms. In so far as … We're not offering to … buy, or …

…

You must have questions.

Beat.

The thought suddenly occurs to JO:

JO: Did you get married?

LIA: What? No?

JO: / Okay …

LIA: You think we have to be married / to have a … ?

JO: No, of course not. I / just wondered …

SIMON: We've never wanted to get / married.

LIA: It's so archaic.

JO: Is it? I'd like to be married, one day.

LIA: Why?

JO: I think it's nice.

>   *Beat.*

LIA: I guess we're both different.

>   [*A compliment*] You look the same.

JO: Please.

LIA: Your skin.

JO: My face is like a smashed window.

LIA: No.

>   Funhouse mirror maybe.

>   JO *laughs.*

>   *Pause.*

JO: I'm trying to see it:

>   You two. As parents.

SIMON: Can't you?

JO: I suppose in a hypothetical …

>   But all this

>   Premeditation.

SIMON: It's not a crime.

LIA: You have to plan it. You don't just have sex once and get pregnant.

JO: That happens all the time / actually.

LIA: Then we must have been very unlucky.

JO: I didn't know you wanted it so … desperately.

LIA: It's normal to want it.

JO: You're not normal. You're exceptional. You're curing cancer.

LIA: I hate it when you say that. I'm not curing—

>   I work on the efficiency of the processes that / are used in the creation of drugs that treat a— (wide variety of diseases)

JO: Yes, yes, the processes I know. You're curing cancer more than novels are, aren't you?

SIMON: Okay.

LIA: Priorities change. People have children.

JO: I know. I'm alive in society.

LIA: Okay, I didn't / mean—

JO: I get all the ads for the kids toys and the fertility treatment and the formula and the mum and baby groups. I've had it shoved down my throat my whole life. The need, the importance, the biological friggin imperative. Seen the film, bought the t-shirt, froze the eggs for chrissake, so I get it.

    I get it. I'm just wrapping my head around: you.

LIA: I didn't ask for your understanding.

JO: Just my eggs.

    Beat.

How would it work?

    If I said yes. You've planned it, so tell me. How would it work. Logistically.

LIA: Well, we'd draw up a contract, of course. We'd pay for all the legal … And we can discuss whatever you want about the pregnancy and—

JO: [*to* SIMON] But it would be your (sperm)

    And my (egg)

    [*To* LIA] And you would (carry it)

LIA: Yes.

JO: …

    Why me?

SIMON: You're very important to us. To both of us.

JO: We aren't speaking. We're not friends.

SIMON: You were such a big part of … You'll always be like family.

JO: But it would be easier, wouldn't it? To get an anonymous donor.

LIA: None of it's / easy.

SIMON: The waitlist is nuts, let alone the …

JO: But … emotionally.

SIMON: We thought it would be … nice, for it to be someone we know.

JO: Nice?

LIA: And after …

SIMON: If it was successful.

LIA: After the birth, we …

Eventually we'd tell them how this happened
and who the … biological …

JO: You'd tell them?

SIMON: If you were okay with it.

JO: I …

SIMON: You could be as involved as you like.

JO: What?

SIMON: If you want to.

JO: I can be involved?

LIA: We're trying to be open to the possibility of—

JO: Like, raising it?

SIMON: If you wanted.

JO: Together?

LIA: Not exactly.

JO: How, then?

SIMON: We're just / asking—

JO: What if I live here?

SIMON: Well.

LIA: No that's—

JO: What if that's what I want? To live here, the three of us. Four, of us.

LIA: We're not proposing some sort of—

JO: What if I wanted to sleep in your bed? What if I was in love with
you? Both of you.

LIA: Okay, this / is serious.

JO: What if I wanted everything? If those were my terms.

SIMON: Do you? / Want that?

LIA: Of course she doesn't.

JO: This is ridiculous.

LIA: It's not a joke. You're / so …

JO: I think you've both—I think you've built this into some sort of
utopian—But this would be a business arrangement at best,
wouldn't it? Not business, not a transaction but, a gift, a one-way,
one-time … thing.

LIA: Okay.

SIMON: We're just saying we know this is a lot and we're open to
however you'd like to approach it.

　　　　If you'd like to approach it.

JO: I don't want a child.

SIMON: Okay. That's fine.

JO: I don't think you're listening.

SIMON: We are.

JO: No, you're not. I don't want to raise it, I don't want to be involved. I don't want to be a mother.

LIA: You wouldn't be a mother.

JO: But it's me. My egg. My genetic material. It's been cleaved from my body and it would be born and grow up and have thoughts and feelings and I won't be its parent but it'll be a little bit of me walking around, all the time. And I don't want that.

LIA: When did you get so biological-determinist?

JO: When did you become a fucking fertility-zombie?

LIA: …

SIMON: Okay, let's not—

LIA: You're so selfish.

JO: Please. Having a child: famously the most selfish thing you can do.

LIA: 'Famously'. I can't believe you still say that. I hate that. It's so self-satisfied.

JO: You want to replicate yourself so you can live forever. That's pretty fucking self-satisfied. At least I'll have the decency to leave when I'm done.

LIA: Nothing means anything to you, does it? You have no idea what it's like to really want something.

JO: Why is what you want worth more than what I do?

LIA: You don't want anything.

JO: I want not to have children. I want not to be a mother. That's my choice.

LIA: It's not a choice, it's an absence.

SIMON: Lia.

JO: Okay. You do whatever you like but don't drag me into this futility, this fucking mania.

    Beat.

LIA: [*to* SIMON] I told you she'd be like this.

SIMON: If you don't … Why did you come?

JO: God, I don't know. Morbid curiosity.

    I'll go.

LIA: Why freeze your eggs?

JO: That's none / of your—

LIA: If you hate all of this so much.

JO: I was brainwashed, wasn't I? I had the money. I wanted the option.

LIA: And now you don't?

JO: Now I don't.

LIA: So give someone else the option.

JO: Why should I?

LIA: Generosity? Human decency? Loyalty?

JO: Loyalty? You stole my fucking boyfriend!

LIA: Fuck's sake, ten years ago!

JO: So you *can* admit it.

LIA: Grow up! You weren't even together.

JO: My ex, then. You were my best friend. You don't do that.

LIA: We were hardly best friends.

JO: What does / that mean?

LIA: Oldest friend, maybe. But we'd barely seen each other. You were busy doing coke with your work mates every weekend and trading all your morals for a bigger salary. You'd become a real capitalist fucking asshole to be honest, I didn't even / think you'd notice.

JO: A second ago I was so fucking special to you.

LIA: You are. No-one fucks me off like you do.

JO: You know, I actually thought if I came here and saw you in person you might apologise. You might be even a little bit contrite.

LIA: I apologised at the time. You can't / keep—

JO: That was an excuse, not an apology.

LIA: I don't have anything to apologise for.

JO: I thought you were asking me for a favour. Don't you need me on side?

LIA: It's a selfless act, Jo. You can't demand emotional payment.

JO: I could at least be treated / with a little respect.

LIA: I'm not going to prostrate / myself for you.

JO: / I didn't say that.

LIA: I'm not going to fucking / beg.

JO: You could stop being such a cunt.

LIA: Fucking hell, I knew / you'd do this.

SIMON: [*knowing what* LIA *is about to reveal*] / Lia.

JO: Could be a little / bit grateful.

LIA: Lord it / over us.

JO: Eyeing up my genetics / the second I walk in the door.

LIA: Think you're so / fucking special.

SIMON: / Lia.

JO: Aren't I?

LIA: Fuck off.

SIMON: / Lia!

JO: You want my baby / pretty fucking bad.

LIA: You're not the only person we're asking!

> *Pause.*

JO: …

SIMON: Jo.

JO: Fuck this.

SIMON: No, wait, please.

JO: I can't believe you.

SIMON: Please stay.

JO: 'You're our last chance'?

SIMON: That wasn't a lie.

JO: You're right. I don't know why I'm here.

SIMON: It wasn't totally a lie. Please just give us five more minutes.

LIA: I shouldn't have said that. That was

> If you can just let us …

SIMON: Please.

> *Beat.*

> JO *makes an impatient gesture of 'Go on!'*

LIA: My sister wants to help us, but she's a year older than me and we would have to pay to have her eggs harvested and there's no guarantee that it would work.

JO: There's no guarantee that it would work with me.

LIA: No, but my sister is the longer shot.

> Your eggs are already viable.

> And

> It does mean something, it being you. Me and Jen are family of course, but it's not like, not like us

> Like we were.

JO: Thought we'd / drifted apart—
LIA: Can you just let me
     Obviously we'll always
     I will
     Do.
     Love you.
JO: …
LIA: And you're much cheaper.
     We're fucking broke.
     So.
     That's the truth.

5

SIMON *at* JO*'s flat. A few months later.*

SIMON: How do you think you'll die?
JO: Hi Simon. Won't you come in?
SIMON: I've been thinking about it. What do you think? Stroke? Heart
    attack? God, this is a nice place. Did you just get up?
JO: You want coffee, tea or something? Beer?
SIMON: Alcohol, maybe. Maybe alcohol for me.
JO: You don't drink that much. Do you?
SIMON: You said our place looked nice, but look at this place.
JO: I don't think I said that.
SIMON: Did you have a party?
JO: Just a few friends.
SIMON: I can't have you being mad at me. I want to make this right.
JO: We didn't talk for years.
SIMON: But you're angry now. I can't stand it.
JO: You'll get over it.
SIMON: So? How do you think you'll die?
JO: Helicopter crash. Probably.
SIMON: Right.
JO: Skiing accident. Shark attack.
SIMON: Buried alive.
JO: Trampled by cows.
SIMON: Autoerotic asphyxiation.

JO: Are you particularly worried about that?

SIMON: Yes. No.

Death, absolutely. All the time. But especially (at the moment) Aren't you?

JO: No. Why are you (here)—?

SIMON: I used to think you would be the last person I ever saw. On my deathbed.

JO: And now?

SIMON: My partner, probably.

JO: She has a name.

SIMON: My child.

If and when …

It raises the stakes doesn't it? Being a parent.

JO: …

Beat.

SIMON: I'll probably still think about you too though. Is that okay?

JO: Your thoughts are your own.

SIMON: I really want us / to—

JO: The last person I ever see will probably be a doctor. Or a nurse, actually. It's the nurses that are there, isn't it? The doctors come in and say 'whoops nothing more we can do' but it's the nurses that stay around for the … sticky end.

When my mum died, she'd been in palliative care for a couple months so the nurses knew her and at the end I was there crying and I looked over and the nurse was crying too. Like openly, tears streaming down, more than me.

SIMON: That / seems …

JO: I thought god, how are you so invested? Was my mum really great or are you like this with everyone? Because you must see a lot of people go. You can't take all that on. I mean, you're killing yourself.

Still, I hope my final nurse cries.

SIMON: They won't. You're very rude. They'll be waving you off if anything.

JO: My last thought'll be 'fuck's sake, squeeze out a tear, Simon' then poof, oblivion.

SIMON: Simon?

JO: That's the nurse's name.

SIMON: Cancer. Nothing dramatic. Probably just cancer.

JO: People die of cancer.

SIMON: Your mum.

JO: Everyone dies of cancer.

SIMON: Do you miss her?

JO: I don't know. Sometimes. The symbol anyway, a mother to turn to.

SIMON: You weren't close.

JO: A reason. You're looking for a reason.

SIMON: Reason for what?

JO: You think I had an unhappy childhood and that's why. I'll pass it all on.

SIMON: I didn't say that.

   Didn't you?

JO: No.

SIMON: Okay.

JO: It was fine.

SIMON: Yeah, your mum / was really—

JO: She was fine.

SIMON: Fucking nightmare.

JO: Okay. She's dead.

SIMON: She was never home.

JO: She worked three jobs.

SIMON: Fucking nightmare. Your words.

JO: Don't quote me.

   She … did her best.

SIMON: I'm just saying, you raised yourself.

JO: We were close, towards the end, we were much closer. I moved back in for a few months, when she couldn't do stuff for herself.

SIMON: Okay, I didn't … (know). That's great. I'm glad.

   Beat.

JO: I can't give you a reason, Simon.

SIMON: It's easy for you. You've always been so certain. This one straight path. How do you do that? I question everything, everyday. It's this constant noise. I mean, am I old enough to have kids, you know, mature and stable enough? But also am I young enough, healthy enough? And do I have enough money? Am I successful enough? Have I sold enough copies? Shouldn't I be on to my third or fourth book by now? And why don't I own a house? I should own a house, right? If I want to be a real adult. Be a role model to someone. What sort of an example is that setting? And can I even be good at being a dad anyway? Fatherhood, that is big, isn't it? That is huge. That is influencing the rest of someone's life. Am I good enough for that? Will I be kind enough, fun enough, strict enough, selfless enough? What if they don't like me? Or what if they love me and everything's perfect and then something happens to them? Like an accident or … What the hell do I do then, could I ever cope with that sort of grief? And what if something happens to me? Or to Lia, you know losing a parent when you're young, that can mess you up forever. I mean, cancer, yeah, every stomach ache it's like: fuck.

But you …

JO: I don't live without doubts.

SIMON: Even when we were younger. When we were together, when we talked about the future, it was just … clear for you.

JO: You think that's small-minded.

SIMON: I do, a little. Yeah.

JO: So go on. I'm listening. Convince me.

SIMON: I don't have a sell, I …

I can't put it into words there's not any one thing that's … convincing. Just every time I … I've been trying to imagine my life, the rest of my life, without a child, and I … I can't.

Pause.

Why am I here?

JO: You want us to be friends?

SIMON: Yes.

JO: And?

SIMON: And.

JO: It didn't work out with the sister.

SIMON: No. It didn't work out with the sister.

6

LIA *and* SIMON*'s.*

SIMON: I got so much done today. Pages. I was …
    I've really been finding something lately.
LIA: That's great.
SIMON: I don't know what it is. It's like my mind has just (opened up) …
LIA: Do you miss your office?
SIMON: No. The rent wasn't worth it.
LIA: The couch is wrecking your back.
    You could sit at the kitchen table. We could get you an ergonomic chair.
    Or one of those attachments for a normal chair.
SIMON: I'm fine.
LIA: I know you've given up a lot.
SIMON: No. We both have.
LIA: Yes, but your advance. You hate teaching.
SIMON: I don't.
LIA: It stops you writing.
SIMON: It's worth it.
    … I read an interview today, with this writer.
    Do you remember that book I read last year, with the sister? I lent it to you. The brother that died.
LIA: Told backwards.
SIMON: Incredible book.
    She's got a new one coming out and she was talking about writing since having children and listing all the positive things, you know, how her heart and view of the world and strength and resilience and capacity for love have grown. Beyond measure. But she also, she said, that now there are two small children to look after, she doesn't have any time for walking. On her own. You know, after writing, to process and wind down and decompress. No time at all. And that's so important to me, to how I work, at the moment, so
    I was just thinking. How I'll adapt.
LIA: Simon …

SIMON: You know, when we …
LIA: I don't think you'll have to worry about adapting.
SIMON: I want to.
LIA: I mean …

> She steels herself.

> We should probably
> Talk.

> Beat.

SIMON: We don't have to give up yet.
LIA: I'm so tired.
SIMON: We'll be okay. I love you.
LIA: I love you too. But
> Will the two of us … will it always feel like there's something
> (missing) … ?
SIMON: …

7

JO's flat.

LIA: Do you remember at uni, how we always said that if one of us had
a child, we'd both raise it? In that house. We'd make a baby's room
in the corner of the lounge, and we'd hope it grew up to have your
intelligence and my resilience and a left eye like mine and a right
eye like yours and we never really talked about who the dad would
be or where or why, it was just this vision, this paradise really; no
men, just you and me and a baby.

> Beat.

JO: Do remember at uni, how we'd do ketamine off a toilet seat?

> LIA laughs.

LIA: Okay.
> Fuck.
> You don't give an inch.
JO: I try not to.

> Beat.

I'm glad you called.

LIA: Me too.

JO: Surprised, / but …

LIA: I've been thinking about travelling.

JO: Okay …

LIA: I always thought I'd do more of it. Maybe now's the time.

JO: …

LIA: I've got so much leave piled up.
    Now that we're not saving all of our money for … I can relax a bit.
    Go back to Brazil. For a holiday. Or longer.

JO: I think that's great.

LIA: Or volunteer.
    At a panther sanctuary or an orphanage or
    The orangutans.

JO: You've thought about this.

LIA: Sometimes. I look up programs. Places I'd like to go.

JO: I like that.

LIA: Don't you do that?

JO: Not really.

LIA: I found this convent.

JO: That's extreme.

LIA: Not forever. But you can live there, for a year or … see how they
    exist. It's on a mountain.
    I have a list. Pages.

JO: Dreams dot doc.

LIA: That's uncomfortably close.

JO: What else?

LIA: Antarctica. Easter Island. The Northern Lights.

JO: Okay.

LIA: I've … this is embarrassing, but I've never been to the Great
    Barrier Reef.

JO: That is embarrassing.

LIA: Raft the Grand Canyon. Walk the Camino. Do Mardi Gras in New
    Orleans. The cherry blossoms in Japan. Volcanoes in Iceland. Route
    Sixty-Six on a motorbike. Count turtle eggs on the Galapagos. Teach
    English. Rhino safari. Clean up the ocean. Go on an archaeological
    dig. A silent retreat. Get my pilot's license. Climb Kilimanjaro.
    Build a school. Drink mezcal in Mexico. Swim with sharks. Run up
    something, jump off something, just: drive.

JO: Wow.

LIA: There's more.

JO: Sounds amazing.

LIA: Not that I'd leave work forever. I mean if we're just talking about dreams, I've got them for work as well. More funding, obviously. More people, full equipment upgrade. A whole extra lab, just for my research.

She gasps.

A really nice coffee machine for the staffroom.

JO *laughs.*

What about you?

JO: I don't know.

LIA: You must have a list. A dreams dot doc.

JO: No.

LIA: You must. A pipe dream. If you won the lottery.

JO: … A … gold plated robot that does laundry?

LIA: I'm serious.

JO: So am I.

LIA: You're nuts.

JO: Maybe I'm fulfilled?

LIA: Get fucked.

JO: It's nice to see you like this.

LIA: Like what?

JO: Like you used to be.

LIA: I haven't changed so much.

JO: No, it's good. I want you to … have a good life.

LIA: I do.

JO: It's just good to know you still … want things. Other things.

LIA: I can want things and want children.

JO: I know.

LIA: I mean, I always wanted kids.

JO: Yeah.

Pause.

Not totally / always.

LIA: I knew you were going to say that.

JO: I know too much.

LIA: Yes, always. I just wasn't ready then.

JO: I'm not attacking you.

LIA: I know. I just

> That's a whole other …
>
> I haven't thought about it in years.

JO: I think about it all the time. That was the most adult thing I'd ever done.

LIA: My abortion was the most adult thing you'd ever done?

JO: Going with you.

LIA: I never told anyone else.

JO: Really? In all this time? Not even Simon?

LIA: No.

JO: You don't … feel differently … ?

LIA: No. Not at all. I want a child, I'm not pro-life.

JO: Pro-life. Fuck. That is a masterclass in branding, isn't it?

LIA: Is it?

JO: Not anti-abortion, not anti-women; pro-life. Just to speak professionally, as a person in advertising, that is a hell of a slogan. You almost forget it's the bad one.

LIA: You should see if they've got jobs going.

> *Beat.*

JO: I never told anyone either.

LIA: About me? I hope not.

JO: About me.

LIA: …

JO: I don't know why.

> Maybe I thought people wouldn't be quite as understanding at thirty-three as they are at twenty.
>
> Not that I give a fuck what people think.
>
> Maybe I just
>
> Didn't really have anyone I wanted to tell.
>
> *Pause.*

LIA: You know it's people like you, don't you,

> Intelligent, socially engaged people who should be raising the next generation. You should really think about it.

JO: What the—?

> LIA *grins, she's kidding.*

Oh, fuck offffffffff.

LIA: What? You heard that one?

JO: You're the worst.

LIA: What about caring for something bigger than yourself?

JO: Your heart expanding.

LIA: Seeing the world through innocent eyes.

JO: The joy of existence.

LIA: Unconditional love.

JO: Your legacy.

LIA: Fuck.

JO: It's all so …

LIA: Ego-centric?

JO: Weird I haven't been converted.

LIA: Like a cult.

JO: Exactly.

> *Beat.*

LIA: Jo.

JO: Yeah?

LIA: You can tell me.

JO: What? If I change my mind?

LIA: No.

JO: / Good.

LIA: Anything. You can tell me anything.

JO: Okay.

LIA: We used to tell each other everything.

> I'd like to get back to that.

JO: Yeah. Maybe. Eventually.

LIA: But. If you were in trouble or … something happened.

JO: Sure. / Okay.

LIA: I came to you for help. After all this time. I think that really says something about us, about how we can always be there for each other.

JO: I think you're papering over / some cracks.

LIA: I'm saying I would be there for you.

JO: Okay. Understood.

LIA: Why don't you trust me?

JO: What's trust got / to do with—

LIA: Everything.

JO: What are you / getting at?

LIA: Just tell me what happened.

JO: When?!

LIA: When you froze your eggs!

JO: We've been over this.

LIA: You were sick, weren't you? Just tell me, just tell me you were sick.

JO: … No, / I …

LIA: You see? You don't trust me.

JO: I don't know what you're talking about.

LIA: Yes, you do. I've been thinking about it. I've been turning it over in my head. Lying awake. Because you're a very certain person. You're not easily influenced, you don't err on the side of caution, you don't think you might change your mind, you just jump. And you knew, you've always known, you don't want kids. You don't want an option or a back up so why why would you …

 And then it … just clicked. You: stubborn, single-minded, but … cancer. Like your mum. The only thing that could even possibly change your mind a little. The treatment can affect your fertility so they tell you to freeze your eggs. That's it, that's the only thing that makes sense. I figured it out. You can't hide anything from me. You had cancer. Just fucking tell me.

 Beat.

JO: It didn't change my mind.

LIA: …

JO: I kept telling them, I don't want this. But they are so insistent. 'You don't know how you might feel in the future!' The gaslighting is just … Whatever. I wasn't wavering, I was bored of the argument.

 Total fucking overreaction, I barely even lost my hair.

LIA: You should have told us.

JO: I'm fine now. Everything's fine.

LIA: When was / it?

JO: It doesn't matter.

LIA: Were you with Connor / or—

JO: No, it was before. He knew, / but—

LIA: We could have helped.

JO: I have friends.

LIA: Why wouldn't you say something?

JO: I didn't want to have this conversation.

LIA: / Okay.

JO: I had people, I had support. I didn't need / any—

LIA: Okay.

> Good. That's good.

JO: Take that look off your face.

LIA: I don't have a look. I'm not looking.

JO: Is that why you called?

LIA: No. I don't care. Cancer? Whatever. Get over it.

JO: Right.

LIA: You should celebrate.

JO: I did. I had a remission party.

LIA: But you should go skydiving or something.

JO: You are obsessed with activities!

LIA: It's fun!

JO: You go skydiving. You have the time of your life.

LIA: Maybe I will.

JO: Good.

LIA: Maybe I'll go tomorrow.

JO: Maybe this is the best thing that's ever happened to you.

LIA: A new start.

JO: Brave new world.

LIA: Dystopian?

JO: Freeing!

LIA: Maybe.

JO: Seriously, you'll look back on this as a turning point.

LIA: Yeah …

JO: The day your life changed.

LIA: Right.

JO: The day you escaped. The day you dodged bullet.

LIA: / Okay …

JO: I mean this is a fucking godsend if you think about it.

LIA: / Not a—

JO: The stress, the sleepless nights, the weight gain …

LIA: / Please …

JO: It's all so shit—

LIA: / Stop …

JO: I mean, who would fucking want that?

> *Beat.*

> LIA *breaks down.*

Sorry, I … Fuck. No. Sorry I, thought we were …
Fuck. I'm sorry.
Oh god. Please stop.

> *Maybe* JO *almost starts to cry here.*

Please. I can't bear it.

LIA: I do. I want / that.

JO: I didn't mean that. I didn't mean to say that.

LIA: It's not shit.

JO: No. Of course. I just meant, you know, the nappies and all the …
But … It's okay. You're okay! What about everything we've talked about? All your dreams.

LIA: This is my dream!

JO: …

LIA: You think I'm pathetic.

JO: I don't.

LIA: You think I'm deluded.

JO: No.

LIA: That I think it'll be all roses and baby powder and little halos or whatever, but I know. I know what it'll be like. No sleep and fluids on every surface and crying and screaming and they'll grow up to be awful and call me names and fucking hate me and leave home and the constant constant doubt are they safe are they happy are they ever going to call?
I know.
And I want all of that.
I want to love someone so much it's like pain, physical pain to be away from them. I want that, I want the pain, I want it to hurt, I want it to kill me.
I'm in pain, anyway.
I'm in pain.

Pause.

JO: I'm sorry.

LIA: No you're not.

JO: It's not easy, to see you hurting.

LIA: You can stop it.

JO: I can't.

LIA: You hate me.

JO: No. I don't.

LIA: You must. Why else would you do this? Take this away from me.

JO: I'm not taking it. You never had it.

LIA: You must fucking despise me. It's my fault. Just admit it.

JO: It's not about you. You're irrelevant.

LIA: Fuck you.

JO: In this. You're irrelevant in this.

LIA: But this *is* me. It's my fault. I messed it all up.

JO: You didn't. Biology's fucked, it's not / you—

LIA: Not that. Us. You've never forgiven me for Simon.

JO: What?

LIA: And your mum. For not being at the funeral.

Beat. Maybe this is closer to it.

JO: …

LIA: I thought that you wouldn't want me there, with everything, that I'd … I don't know, detract from your grief or something. I thought seeing me might make it … worse? Which is obviously so … (absurd) But I should have been there for you. I'm sorry. / I'm really—

JO: Please don't apologise.

LIA: No. It's not okay. I know that. You were my best friend and I wasn't there for you, I didn't come to your mum's funeral and I stole your boyfriend and I couldn't give Simon a baby and I've neglected my research and, I mean, maybe I could have fucking cured cancer and maybe your mum wouldn't be dead and none of us would be miserable and it's me it's my fault I'm the rot at the centre I'm fucking broken I'm—

JO: I slept with Simon.

LIA: … What?

JO: After the funeral.

LIA: … No you didn't.

JO: I was grieving.

> And I hated you. Yes, for not being there. For everything.
> That whole time is kind of a blur but
> The … My abortion.
> I never told him. I thought about it. I called. But in the end I …
> I didn't know you were trying for a baby.
> I don't know if that would have made a difference, but I like to think I wouldn't have been that cruel on purpose.
> Or maybe I would.
> So.
> Now you can hate me.

> *Pause. Perhaps a long one. Eventually:*

> Are you … going to say anything?

LIA: It's fine.

JO: … Why?

LIA: I hurt you. Now you've hurt me.

JO: So what … we're even?

> LIA *shrugs and looks away.* JO *goes to put her hand on* LIA*'s, but pulls back.*

> *Long beat.*

LIA: I should go.

JO: No, don't. I want to tell you (why) …

> *Beat.*

LIA: What?

JO: …

> JO *can't say it.*

LIA: Okay.

> LIA *turns to go.*

JO: Jelly for arms or risotto for legs?!

> *Beat.*

LIA: …

JO: Arms, right? No brainer.

LIA: Help me understand. If you want me to have a good life. Help me be like you. Help me not care. Help me not to want it.

JO: I don't know how.

LIA: Tell me what you're going to do.

JO: About what?

LIA: About your life.

   With the rest of your life.

JO: Whatever I want.

LIA: Right. Right, but …

   You like your life?

JO: Yes.

LIA: But what is it?

JO: Maybe you *should* go.

LIA: Tell me!

JO: I don't know what / you— (want, mean)

LIA: You don't really like your career that much.

JO: I like my career.

LIA: But you're not passionate about it. You're not dedicated to it.

JO: I'm dedicated to it forty hours a week. I do a / good job.

LIA: You wanted to be a writer.

JO: Look at my couch though. It's so nice.

LIA: You give up on things.

JO: I chose security. I never had that. So I chose it for myself.

LIA: But what are you going to do? What else is there to do?

JO: Anything. Anything I want.

LIA: You said yourself you're not interested in travelling.

JO: I'm interested in going on holiday.

LIA: You don't have a bucket list.

JO: Neither do you. Not one you actually plan on doing.

LIA: But you could. You could do those things. You have time, you have money. No-one depends on you.

JO: People do depend on me. People would notice if I was dead. Just because I didn't grow them in my own body.

LIA: But you could dedicate your life to a cause or go back to / school or—

JO: Yeah great, I'll just go live in a convent.

LIA: But what are you going to do otherwise?

JO: Who the fuck are you?

LIA: Answer me. You owe me this.

JO: I don't owe you shit.

LIA: Just fucking answer.

JO: Nothing! If those are the options, maybe just nothing then.

LIA: You can't do nothing.

JO: Why? Because I'm not dedicating my life to children, I have to dedicate it to something else? I must lose my life to something?

LIA: Yes! Yes, you have to do something. We all do.

JO: Then I'll sleep! I'll … I don't know. I'll sleep more.

> LIA *scoffs*.

I like to sleep. I like to sleep in. I'd like to do that more. I like to wake up without an alarm or a baby crying. I like realising it's Saturday and I can do whatever I want. I like going to the café where they know me and drinking a coffee in the sun and watching people go about their day without time pressure, without anywhere I need to be. Without obligatory hobbies or activities or community fucking service.

I like the things that everyone likes. I don't want to be special or interesting, I want to do the easy everyday things that everyone wishes they had more time for. I want to meet friends, go for walks, read a book, eat cake, have a nap, watch hours of TV, plant things that may or may not grow, drink a really good glass of wine. I like being able to book a last-minute holiday or drop everything to help someone or …

Last weekend a friend from work called me at ten p.m. because she was at a bar round the corner and I met her for a beer and we ended up at some stranger's house party and we talked for hours to everyone about everything and nothing and I didn't get home till the sun was up and I can do that. I can do that if I want to.

And I like making dinner now. That's new. I went to a hen's night cookery class and I discovered I like, I really like, making my own pastry. That's how old I am. Puff pastry. It's this fucking laborious thing, you have to keep folding and folding and putting it in the fridge and then folding again. I really like the satisfaction of that. You make a pie with your own pastry. Maybe one day with vegetables that you grew yourself. That's really living for me. Lia, I make my own croissants!

I want to have more days where I can do whatever I want. Where I can do nothing, if I want. I want every day to be Saturday. That's the life I want.

Beat.

LIA: But what does that mean?

JO: I don't want it to mean anything! I'm not important, I don't need a legacy. You're not listening.

LIA: I am.

JO: No, you're obliterating me. I'm trying so hard to see you and hear you and understand what you want and why it matters. And I am just nothing to you. I don't exist.

LIA: You do, I … I care. I want you to have a good life, too.

I want to know …

JO: … What?

LIA: … When someone asks you. When you're dying,

JO: I'm not dying!

LIA: I know! But when you are. In thirty years, in a hundred years.

When someone says 'what did you do with your life?' What will you have to show for it?

JO: Lia, nothing's perfect. No-one has everything.

LIA: But what will you say?

JO: I'll say I was happy.

I'll say I had such a nice time.

8

JO *'s place.* JO *and* SIMON *are drunk.*

JO: I never go to that bar anymore.

SIMON: Me neither.

JO: You chose it.

SIMON: I was just walking and ended up there.

JO: We used to go there all the time.

SIMON: I was thinking about you.

JO: You said.

SIMON: Is it okay that I called?

JO: You don't need to keep asking me that.

SIMON: So, it is?

JO: I had a nice night.

SIMON: It's good to not talk about serious things.

JO: I'm very non-serious.

SIMON: I like your place.

JO: You said.

SIMON: It's very you.

JO: Cold?

SIMON: Clean. Open. Lots of shiny fittings.

> JO *laughs.*

I missed your laugh.

JO: No you didn't.

SIMON: How drunk are you?

JO: I don't know.

> Enough.

> *Beat. He kisses her.*

SIMON: Fuck, you're beautiful.

> SIMON *goes to kiss her again, but she can't help sniggering.*

Okay, I didn't miss that laugh.

JO: Sorry, sorry, it's just … Such a line.

SIMON: It's not a line. You are.

JO: Yes, I know.

SIMON: I was just trying to be …

JO: What? Romantic?

SIMON: You're so defensive.

JO: You're so tacky.

SIMON: You suggested coming back.

JO: Yeah. Well.

> This isn't very original, is it?

SIMON: You want me to go?

JO: No.

* * *

The next morning.

JO: Oh fuck. Oh fuck fuck fuck fuck.

SIMON: Morning to you too.

JO: Oh fuck what is wrong with me? What the fuck is fucking wrong with me?

SIMON: It's okay.

JO: No it's not, it's not okay I'm a horrible person, I'm disgusting, I'm scum, I hate myself so much.

SIMON: / It's okay, Jo.

JO: How could I do this to her again?

SIMON: You haven't done anything.

JO: I have I have I—fuck, will you tell her?

SIMON: No.

JO: Okay.

    Okay.

    That's an answer. That's a definite—

    Shouldn't you?

    I mean, maybe we should, together, you know, confess or—

SIMON: It wouldn't do anyone any good.

JO: Wouldn't it? Won't she ask questions? Won't you need to explain where you've been?

SIMON: We broke up.

JO: … What? When?

SIMON: A few weeks ago.

JO: Why?

SIMON: Because it's over.

    Because it's over.

JO: You didn't tell me.

SIMON: I know.

JO: Why the fuck wouldn't you tell me? All last night.

SIMON: I was going to I … I thought it might be strange.

    I didn't want you to think I was expecting something.

JO: Expecting what?

SIMON: Sex? An apology?

    / I don't know.

JO: An apol—? Was it about me?

SIMON: No? Not everything's about you.

    Beat.

JO: You should have told me.

SIMON: This is better, isn't it?

    That we've broken up.

    I mean, that I'm …

    technically

    single.

JO: Yes. Is it? I don't know.

SIMON: You'd prefer that I was cheating on her?

JO: Of course not.

    This is just … different.

    It just would have been nice to know.

* * *

A couple weeks later.

SIMON: Really?

JO: Yeah, I just, I feel weird so …

SIMON: No, of course we can stop, that's totally

    Are you okay?

JO: I'm fine. I might shower.

SIMON: Because I said … ?

JO: Yeah.

SIMON: But you … you like it when I say that.

JO: Yeah, this is me liking it.

SIMON: You used to like it.

JO: It used to not mean anything.

SIMON: It doesn't mean … it's doesn't have to mean anything now.

JO: Really?

SIMON: I was in the moment.

JO: You 'want to cum inside me'?

SIMON: Okay. You don't have to repeat it / back to me.

JO: That doesn't mean anything?

SIMON: You used to think it was hot.

JO: I used to be twenty-two.

Beat.

You know you've never even asked me if I'm on birth control, don't you?

SIMON: Alright. I'm sorry. I'm an arsehole, okay? Is that what you want to hear?

Beat.

You are, right? On birth control?

JO: …

SIMON: No, okay, that's … I'm sorry. Really. I wasn't thinking. I wasn't thinking about babies. I was thinking about you and us and I've fucking missed you all week and I just felt really close to you and I know, obviously, in retrospect that was kind of a … fraught thing to say but I have really just made this total block in my mind between you know, trying to have a baby and … what we were just … I know that probably isn't healthy but, you know, because it's like one you talk to your mum about and the other you … don't. So. I'm sorry.

Beat.

JO *laughs.*

What?

JO: I'm just imagining you talking to your mum about this.

SIMON: Ugh. Okay. Shut up.

JO: You missed me?

SIMON: You know, a little.

JO: All week, you said.

SIMON: Maybe.

JO: You like me.

SIMON: Nah.

JO: You love me.

SIMON: Psh.

JO: [*annoying singing*] You wanna hug me.

SIMON: / Whatever.

JO: You wanna kiss me. You wanna cum inside—

SIMON *puts his hand over* JO'*s mouth before she can finish her sentence.*

SIMON: [*gently*] Shut. Up.

> *He takes his hand away. They kiss.*

* * *

A few days later.

SIMON: I've just realised.
>   This is our bed.
JO: It's my bed.
SIMON: Was our bed. The bed we bought together.
JO: I just really love this frame, okay? It's mid-century and we got it
    for a steal.
>   I got a new mattress.
SIMON: You burn the old one?
JO: Because I was updating. Not as a symbolic gesture.
SIMON: Clean slate's not a bad idea though.
JO: I don't buy a new mattress for each new sexual partner, that'd be—
SIMON: Unhinged.
JO: Expensive.
SIMON: How expensive?
JO: Shut up.
SIMON: If beds could talk.
JO: It is memory foam.

> *They laugh.*

SIMON: I've been sleeping on a futon for a decade.
JO: That's very sad.
SIMON: Lia was always saying we should get a memory foam.
>   Sorry.
JO: Are you talking?
SIMON: Sometimes. There's stuff to deal with. House stuff.
JO: How is she?
SIMON: She's good. She's good. She's
>   It's hard, you know.
JO: Do you miss her?
SIMON: Yes. I do.
JO: Does she know about us?

SIMON: No.

JO: Does she say anything? About me.

SIMON: Like what?

JO: Like she hates me.

SIMON: No.

JO: Like she wishes I was dead. Like she hopes I choke on my own fertile fucking loins.

SIMON: She doesn't say stuff like that.

JO: No. Fucking saint.

SIMON: Don't get me wrong, she's not just … mourning. She has a very full life.

JO: Activities.

SIMON: Right, right. I was always jealous of that.

JO: What about you? Are you mourning?

SIMON: I'm fine.

JO: But you wanted / a

SIMON: Yes.

> And, eventually …

JO: You've got time.

SIMON: Right. Yeah, I …

> No. God, I'm sick to death of hearing that actually.
>
> Just because I physically can—and that's a whole other (thing) because male fertility is rapidly declining anyway—but okay, so assuming I physically can, doesn't mean that I
>
> I don't want to be a new dad at fifty, okay? I want to enjoy the
>
> I want to be fit and healthy for their, and you know, *alive* for their
>
> Sorry. We don't have to …
>
> I have time. More time than
>
> It's a privilege. I know that.
>
> *Beat.*

JO: Do you think I'm cruel?

SIMON: I think you're wonderful.

> *Beat.*

JO: You know we're not back together, don't you?

SIMON: … I know.

JO: I mean that would be ridiculous. For both of us. And.
    I would never do that.
    To Lia.
SIMON: … Wouldn't you?

9

LIA *'s place.* JO *has come over.*

LIA: Why now?
JO: I feel bad.
LIA: About what?
JO: …
LIA: I don't want your pity eggs.
JO: Yes you do.
LIA: Beggars can't be choosers?
JO: You never begged. Actually.
LIA: I know Simon told you about the break-up, so … We aren't going
    to (get back together).
JO: / Yeah. I know.
LIA: Even if there was a baby. I'd get a donor. I'd raise them by myself.
JO: I'm not anti-single mothers, am I? I had a single mother.
LIA: And you turned out great.
JO: Do you want them or not?
LIA: [*vulnerable*] What if you change your mind again?
JO: I won't.
LIA: How do I know that?
JO: Because when you first asked me, I was hurt. And I'm not now.
LIA: Hurt about what?
JO: … About you. After all this time. You asking me …

I'd just had this big break-up, with Connor. Because he wanted
kids. And he knew I didn't, he'd always known, I've always been
very honest about it. But he wanted us to have a baby together.
He thought I would change my mind. He said we would be good
parents, that I would be a good mother, that our kid would be cute
and smart and, you know, save the world. And I wished I could give
him what he wanted. But I felt sick every time he talked about it
because I knew I couldn't. I knew eventually I'd have to tell him no,

no I won't change my mind. I'll never … Even though it'd break his heart. Break my (heart) …

And then, you. Like a week after we broke up you crash back into my life asking for the same fucking thing. And all I could think was: why is that all anyone wants from me? Why is that the only thing about me worth anything? Even to you. Why isn't just me enough … ?

LIA: I don't think that's the only thing about you / worth anything—

JO: Right.

But in ten years, it's the only reason you called.

LIA: I never meant—

JO: I know.

LIA: I'm sorry.

Beat.

JO: There's no rules. That's the problem. There's no rules for this. No rituals. I used to think we'd spend our lives together. We didn't need children, or husbands, we had each other. But there's no fucking rituals. There's no marriage, there's no break ups. You just drift apart, just stop speaking. There's no mourning, no socially acceptable breakdown or sympathy. It's fucked. I want to sign a document. Let me preserve this acrimony for future generations. It doesn't matter how many new friends you make … I deserve, *we* deserve, a marker, a memorial. I want to get to say: I'm divorced. I want to tell everyone, I had this One Great Friendship.

LIA: …

JO: Yeah. So anyway, the eggs might be a bit pre-disposed to cancer. And depression, obviously. But that's everyone, isn't it? And there's arthritis on my mum's side. And heart stuff on my dad's, I think. Heartlessness, anyway. Joking. But, not funny. So they're yours if you want them. Bit imperfect, but they're free. There's a dozen of them, actually. Which *is* kind of funny. And I don't want them, so yeah. Maybe you're right, I should give them to someone.

Maybe she can't look at LIA *when she says this.*

To someone I love.

Beat.

LIA: Okay.

JO: Okay?

LIA: Thanks.

JO: [*exaggeratedly casual*] Yeah, no worries.

LIA: Should we do something? Formal?

JO: Well, there's a whole process. Forms and / all the legal—

LIA: Yes, I just thought we should do something now. A ritual?

JO: / Okay.

LIA: Like a … gentleman's agreement.

> JO *laughs, then* LIA *joins in.*

JO: A gentleman's … ?

LIA: I don't know.

JO: Do you have your own quill?

> *They are both really laughing now.*

LIA: Shut up.

JO: I brought parchment, but I was hoping you'd provide the wax seal and yoke of oxen yourself.

> *They calm.*

LIA: I hate you.

> LIA *offers her hand to shake.* JO *hugs her.*

10

A year or so later. A supermarket.

SIMON: Jo.

JO: … Hi.

SIMON: Hi.

JO: What are you … ? I mean, do you live … ?

SIMON: No! No, I had a meeting. Thought I'd just get some stuff for dinner before the train.

JO: Right. Phew.

SIMON: Yeah. Yeah.

>   How are you?

JO: Yeah, / I'm …

SIMON: How are you doing with … ? It must be weird.

JO: What, that I'm not safe in my own supermarket?

SIMON: No. No I meant
        The baby. What he must be, three months now?
JO: …
SIMON: …
JO: Oh. / Yeah, right—
SIMON: Oh fuck, you didn't know she'd had the baby.
JO: I didn't know she was pregnant.
SIMON: Oh. Shit.
JO: I asked not to be told anything.
SIMON: Fuck. Sorry.
JO: No, it's
        It's fine.
SIMON: Now I've made it weird.
JO: It's not weird.
        I'm—
        Good for her.
SIMON: Yeah, she's / really—
JO: I don't want to talk about it.
SIMON: Okay.
JO: How are you?
SIMON: I'm good. I'm great.
JO: Great.
        … Well,
SIMON: I submitted the manuscript.
JO: Oh. Congratulations. When does it … ?
SIMON: It's still early drafts so, not for a while but
        My agent is very excited. And the publisher. I think it's better
    than my last one.
        How's your work? Did you write that ad for the chocolate bar?
    The strawberry …
JO: I did.
SIMON: I can still recognise your tone.
JO: What an achievement.
SIMON: I think that's something. That your voice comes through.
JO: Only to the trained ear.
SIMON: I'm seeing someone.
JO: … Okay. Great.

SIMON: You?
JO: Yeah.

> *Beat.*

SIMON: She's an editor. Alana.
> She's great.
> She's not my editor but she's
> We met at an industry thing.
> I always thought it was a mistake to be with someone in the same field, but it's actually
> You know, you don't have to explain everything, they just
> Get it.
> And
> We're having a baby.
> I haven't told Lia yet. I'm not avoiding it, I just
> Anyway I'm glad to see you
> To tell you
> First.
> I've been thinking about (you? us?)
> Anyway.
> It's funny
> How things work out.
> I mean

> *This is, at least partially, a lie.*

We all got what we wanted.

11

A couple of years later. LIA*'s place.*

LIA: He's here.
JO: … Oh.
LIA: He's sick, so, day care wouldn't take him.
JO: You didn't say.
LIA: No.
> They're just constantly sick actually and then you get sick and …
> He's sleeping, so you don't have to—
JO: We can do this another / time.

LIA: He'll be asleep for another hour. We just got into a new schedule
and it's really working which is (amazing). People say terrible twos,
but wow, anyway

So you really won't have to see him.

Unless you—

JO: I don't.

LIA: No, so. Coast's clear.

JO: But he's … ?

LIA: Yes.

JO: You should have told me.

LIA: I thought you wouldn't come.

And on the phone you sounded

Like you needed to talk, like there was something—

JO: No, no it's nothing.

I just wanted to see you.

Beat.

LIA: Right.

JO: I thought, with the book coming out …

LIA: Right. Yes.

JO: But there's really not an urgent—

LIA: Jo. Sit down.

JO: … Okay.

LIA: I made coffee. Would you … ?

JO: Thank you.

LIA *gets coffee.*

LIA: So you read it.

JO: Wish I hadn't. Tried not to.

It was the invite to the launch that really made me want to talk
to you.

Just the generic invite, not even a personal

I'm sure you didn't go either.

LIA: [*she did*] No. I didn't.

LIA *changes the subject.*

He got you better in the first one.

JO: I was completely idealised.

LIA: It was spot-on.

To me, anyway.

Except for that one scene.

JO: At your birthday party.

LIA: I hated that.

JO: So naive, like everything was pre-destined. Like he was the centre.

LIA: I don't even remember meeting him then.

JO: You did, but you were mid-throw up at the time.

LIA: How romantic.

JO: Still. Idealised better than demonised. We're all awful in the second one.

LIA: There's a third.

JO: He'll need some new material.

LIA: So you don't … ?

JO: No. You?

LIA: Not for …

Beat.

I'm a little relieved.

JO: About what?

LIA: I thought you two / might be—

JO: Oh no, not at all, he's with / someone and—

LIA: No, not together, I know he's with (Alana)

I meant

Friends, I suppose.

In each other's lives.

I was jealous.

JO: Of what?

LIA: That you could stay friends with him.

You were always more

Forgiving.

JO: Well, it's different.

Beat.

LIA: …

I've been thinking about you.

When I was pregnant I kept thinking you could hear my thoughts. Osmosis or something.

When I saw your name on my phone, I thought I was dreaming it.

JO: In the flesh.

LIA: Yes.

JO: How's it going?
      With … (the baby)

LIA: Good. He's great. Exhausting, but. My sister's been amazing and
    work are so flexible and …

JO: No regrets, then?

LIA: No. God, no.

      Beat.

JO: I don't know the questions to ask.

LIA: You must have friends with kids.

JO: We tend to lose touch.

      Beat.

LIA: I know you don't want me to say thank you but I am
      / So grateful.

JO: No. Sure.

      Beat.

LIA: My dad went into a home.
      Into aged care, I mean. He was … my mum was having to care for
    him, wash him and basically everything and she wasn't coping, so.
    Sorry. I don't know why I wanted to tell you that, but, that's my news.

      Beat.

JO: I got married.

LIA: Oh. Wow. Congratulations.

JO: Yeah, thank you. We're happy. It's good, it's sort of, blissful.

      Beat.

LIA: So, / who's—

JO: I should go.

LIA: No, don't. Stay, I—

JO: I just wanted to / check in but—

LIA: Jo, on the phone you sounded
      You were so clear about
      Not wanting any contact.

JO: I know.

Maybe I'm getting old. Nostalgic, I don't know.

But you seem good / so—

LIA: It's come back, hasn't it?

Beat.

JO: Nice coffee.

LIA: Hasn't it?

JO: What do you use, a stovetop or … ?

LIA: Is there treatment?

JO: … Lia.

LIA: There is treatment. There's a plan.

JO: Yeah, yeah, there's a plan.

LIA: Okay, good. That's good.

JO: …

Beat.

LIA: It's a drip machine.

JO: Right.

LIA: Probably the most expensive thing in the house.

JO: Good investment.

LIA: Do you want to see him? I can wake him up. It's not such / a big deal.

JO: No. No.

I told you, I didn't …

I wanted to see you, not (him)—

Beat.

LIA: Maybe next time?

JO: Yeah, maybe.

LIA: I'm sorry.

JO: Don't be.

LIA: Do you

Have … people?

JO: Yes. I do.

LIA: Oh. Yes, you said your husband and um. Good. That's good.

JO: And you're not one of those freaks that loves the smells of hospitals are you, anyway, so. I'll let you get on. There must be lots you have to do.

LIA: Always. Laundry's fucking
　　　Endless.
　　　Have you got somewhere to be?
JO: Yeah. Well, no. I'm taking a sort of sabbatical from work so …
LIA: Every day's Saturday.
JO: Exactly.

　　　JO *heads for the door.* LIA *stands too.*

LIA: I am. One of those freaks, for hospitals. Disinfectant and urine,
　　　I love it. I'm a total … pervert for hospitals.

　　　JO *stifles a laugh.*

JO: Okay, fine.
LIA: You'll call?
JO: Yeah.
LIA: Promise me.
JO: … I promise.
LIA: You don't have to
　　　Rush off.
JO: I know.
　　　I want to.

THE END

Red Stitch THE ACTORS' THEATRE

presents

What's Yours

26 JULY – 24 AUGUST, 2025

Playwright
Keziah Warner

Director
Isabella Vadiveloo

Set and Costume Design
Bianca Pardo

Lighting Design
Rachel Lee

Composition/Sound Design
Grace Ferguson and Ethan Hunter

Stage Manager
Jessica Smart

Assistant Stage Manager
Ella Thompson

Simon – **Kevin Hofbauer**
Lia – **Carissa Lee**
Jo – **Christina O'Neill**

Hansen Graduate Assistant Director – **Roisin Wallace Nash**

Hansen Graduate Attachment – **Sookyung Shin**

This play was developed through Red Stitch's INK writing program.

Red Stitch THE ACTORS' THEATRE

Established in 2001, Red Stitch is Australia's leading acting ensemble.

Our home space of 80 seats in St Kilda has produced critically lauded theatre for 24 years, with over 175 productions to our name, contributing to our reputation as a leading commissioner and producer of exceptional Australian theatre. Our INK program sustains the increased representation of Australian drama in the national repertoire, supporting an illustrious coalition of playwrights and artists. Nineteen Australian plays have been produced, one third of which have toured nationally or internationally. Our biennial site-specific festival of music and new writing, PLAYlist, has attracted a large and loyal audience and a vibrant reputation in the community.

Our determination to create a pathway for emerging artists to traverse the challenging transition from tertiary institutions to the professional sector led the company to establish the Red Stitch Graduate program in 2008. Today the Hansen Graduate Program supports five early career practitioners annually, offering young artists the opportunity to work with the company throughout the year across a range of disciplines gaining vital hands-on experience. This has in turn furnished the company with fresh perspectives and ideas.

Current Artistic Director/CEO, Ella Caldwell, oversees a company in which over 60 artists have occupied ensemble positions, with 12-15 advisors active at any time and membership refreshed annually. Several original ensemble members hold advisory positions and regularly return to work with the company along with guest artists who bring their vision, talent and energy to the company.

Red Stitch is a resilient, constantly evolving and uniquely creative company, earning recognition and awards alongside much better funded high profile counterparts. As a crucial bridge between independent practice and larger institutions, our artists evolve and hone their craft while simultaneously generating exceptional work for audiences.

Red Stitch has earned a treasured place in the theatre-going community of Melbourne and contributed significantly to the national culture.

Thank you for joining us.

Artistic Director/CEO
Ella Caldwell

Production and Technical Manager
Charlie Bowyer

Front-of-House Manager
Penelope Thomson

Producer
Krystalla Pearce

Marketing Coordinator
Darcy Kent

Finance Manager
Shadi Habash

RED STITCH ENSEMBLE

Lucy Ansell
Jacob Battista
Ella Caldwell
Richard Cawthorne
Jing-Xuan Chan
Jessica Clarke
Kate Cole
Brett Cousins
Ngaire Dawn Fair
Daniel Frederikson
Emily Goddard
Kevin Hofbauer
Justin Hosking
Khisraw Jones-Shukoor

Darcy Kent
Caroline Lee
Olga Makeeva
Dion Mills
Christina O'Neill
Tim Potter
Ben Prendergast
Kat Stewart
Sarah Sutherland
Andrea Swifte
David Whiteley
Sophie Woodward
Harvey Zielinski

BOARD

We at Red Stitch acknowledge and pay our respects to Australia's First Peoples and Elders past and present, and offer our gratitude to the Boon Wurrung and Wurundjeri Woi Wurrung peoples of the Kulin Nation, on whose unceded lands we work.

THANK YOU

This development and production of *What's Yours* would not have been possible without the generous support of our donors and partners

KINDRED DONORS

Maureen Wheeler AO & Tony Wheeler AO

Ms Jane Hansen AO

Andrew Domasevicius SLD & Aida Tuciute

Carrillo Gantner AC & ZiYin Gantner AC

Brenda Joyce

Peter Bartholomew

Beecher Family Charitable Trust, a Sub-Fund of the Australian Communities Foundation

Per & Ingrid Carlsen

Sage Custodians

Jane & Stephen Hains & Portland House Foundation

Graham & Judy Hubbard

Myer Foundation

Anonymous

Anthony Adair

Beth Brown

Sam Frey

The Eric and Elizabeth Gross Foundation

Joanna Murray-Smith AO

The Neff Family

Jenny Schwarz In Memoriam

KSS Foundation

Rosemary Walls

Diana Burleigh

Coote Family Lawyers

Anthony & Susan Dickinson

Michael Kingston

Halina Lewenberg Charitable Foundation

Kate Langbroek on behalf of The Lewis Langbroek Charitable Endowment

Mark O'Dwyer

Craig Reeves

Fiona Symonds

Richard Brettell & Robyn Trevaskis

Christine Turner

Margaret & Peter Yuill

Larry Abel

Anonymous

APS Foundation

Anita & Graham Anderson

Ella Caldwell

Robin Carter
Julie & Ian Cattlin
Nola Daley
Richard Dammery
Anne Donegan
Edwina Mary Lampitt in Memoriam
Damon & Lorena Healey
Linda Herd
Tony Hillery
Akhilesh Jain
Dr George Klempfner
KCL Law
Barbara Long
Lyngala Foundation
Lousie Manson
Patricia Mason
Angela & Peter Matkovic
Kaylene O'Neil
Donna Pelka
Ralph Renard
Timothy Roman
Victoria Rowell
Jenny Ryssenbeek
Simon Schofield
Marshall Segan
James H Syme
Jane Thompson
Peter Veevers & Jenny Veevers
Tony War & Gail Ryan
Graham Webster & Teri Snowdon
Jane Whiting AM

MAJOR PARTNERS

Creative Victoria
Cybec Foundation
City of Port Phillip
Malcolm Robertson Foundation
The Myer Foundation
Sidney Myer Fund
Copyright Agency Cultural Fund
Lyngala Foundation
Playking Foundation
Seaborn, Broughton & Walford Foundation

Rear 2 Chapel Street, St Kilda East, VIC 3183
http://redstitch.net/ | FB: @RedStitchTheatre | T: @redstitch
boxoffice@redstitch.net | 03 9533 8083

PLAYWRIGHT'S NOTES

I always struggle to write a Writer's Note. What can or should I say that (hopefully) the play isn't already saying itself? What if I say something here that undermines everything we've worked so hard on? But this Writer's Note has left me particularly sleepless.

The politicisation of women's choices has had me agonised throughout this play's development. My own internalised judgements have all come raging to the surface at one time or another. At every turn I questioned the decisions I was making for Jo and Lia. Does this word/action/choice make Jo seem heartless? Does this one make Lia seem tragic? Should Lia be more ambitious? Can Jo be independent but not lonely, happy but not delusional, caring but not a carer? Should they be smarter or funnier? Should they be less… everything?

Simon didn't warrant nearly as much scrutiny.

It's right to carefully consider a character's actions, particularly when the content is so personal — not just to me, to everyone. But Jo has especially plagued me. In my search for inspiration,

I read as much fiction as I could find on women who choose to be childfree and I kept coming up against the same problem: the twist at the end. In some cases, that she actually does become a mother and that's what she has secretly wanted all along. And in others, she becomes a mother in some other way, a step-mother, a carer, a pet parent. More than once, I threw these books at the wall. Could Jo's ending ever satisfy everyone?

One of the basic tenets of drama is that your characters have to want something. With motherhood as the societal norm, Jo could be accused (as Lia says) of wanting nothing. Or, wanting not something. Not to be a mother (how dare she). But she does, of course, want lots of things. To put it in her own simple terms, she wants to be happy, to have a nice time. What more can one ask? But is that… dramatic?

What we discovered through development is that the wanting or not wanting a child isn't the point. The baby stuff was the premise of course, but the heart and soul of the play is Jo and

Lia's friendship. And what they both want — at times much much more subconsciously than others - through the fights and the barbs and the jokes and tears, is to repair their One Great Friendship. If you're the sort to wonder what happens after a play ends, it might be nice to imagine they get there, agonised as it might be.

So have I done Jo and Lia justice? I've tried and I hope so, but everyone will bring their own judgement. In our final development just a few days ago I was met with extremely justified laughter when I said 'I know this is quibbling but...' and inserted a comma between the words 'yeah' and 'you' — just to make sure the line wasn't 'interpreted wrong'. So please know this: the trying has been agony.

Thank you to everyone who has agonised with me. Thank you for the support, feedback, nurture and enthusiasm. Ella, Krystalla and the Red Stitch team. Our actors: Chrissy, Kev, Carissa, Emily, Darcy, Jing-Xuan, Brigid, Alice, John Marc. My early and late stage readers: Bridget, Jamaica, Emily, Maddie. And finally to Bella, for the radical empathy, the reassurance, the vision, the debriefs and the croissants.

This play is for everyone who has ever thought about having or not having children. Which is to say, for everyone. And it's dedicated to all the One Great Friendships, divorced or otherwise. We couldn't have done it without them.

Keziah Warner
Playwright

DIRECTOR'S NOTES

Lately when working with designers, I've noticed a habit developing. It begins with an apology: 'I'm going to throw a lot of ideas at you and they'll contradict each other a lot, and then I need you to try and make it make sense… sorry'. With *What's Yours*, my thoughts were clearer but no less contradictory, I kept returning the pull between the intimate and the epic, always reaching, trying to capture both adequately. This was a tension that existed outside of design conversations too — long discussions with Keziah and many brilliant actors and theatre makers took place though development workshops as we debated single words being used to describe characters.

In many ways, the scale of this work is truly epic. Its content is highly political as reproductive rights are thrust firmly back into public discourse and birth rates in Australia plummet, the way we depict people (especially women) 'desperate' for a child or desperate for a life without a child provokes charged responses. We traverse decades with these characters, through a landscape of death, love, birth, ketamine snorted off toilet seats, illness, sex, chaos and stillness. But just as loudly, the intimacy of this work erupts, demanding deep connections depicted with complexity and familiarity. The friendship between Jo and Lia centres this play, and the tremendous pain and euphoria all three characters inflict on each other knocks the air from my lungs every time I read it. A sharp intake of breath, a stumbled line, a loaded pause becomes at once an epic tragedy and a quiet heartbreak.

All of this is the case of course, because Keziah Warner is a very, very good writer. Watching her work is an incredible lesson in vision, collaboration, perceptiveness, humour and emotional intelligence. Her ability to distil an hour-long conversation with a thousand contradicting opinions and complex thoughts into four lines of acerbic dialogue is like a magic trick. Similarly, having the immense privilege of watching actors work continues to be a career perk I can't ever seem to get my head around. Cast members Christina O'Neill, Kevin Hofbauer and Carissa Lee have brought unfathomable generosity, vulnerability and joy to this process, and the impact of actors who worked on the many developments and readings we did in the lead up to the season, Emily Goddard and arcy Kent in particular, lives and breathes in how I've approached directing this play. If there's a theatre company in this city who can claim any kind of expertise in the tension between the epic and the intimate, it must be Red Stitch. Thank you, Ella and the Red Stitch team, for your unwavering support of this work, for the time, space, trust and care.

Isabella Vadiveloo
Director

KEZIAH WARNER
PLAYWRIGHT

Keziah is a playwright and dramaturg. She is currently under commission with the National Institute of Dramatic Art and is the New Work Associate – Script Development at Malthouse Theatre. Previously, she has won Sydney Theatre Company's Patrick White Playwrights Award, been nominated for an AWGIE Award, shortlisted for the Shane & Cathryn Brennan Prize, the Griffin Award, the Martin-Lysicrates Prize, the Rodney Seaborn Playwrights Award, the Max Afford Award and the Lysicrates Prize, highly commended in the Victorian Premier's Literary Awards and longlisted for Soho Theatre's Young Writers Award. Her writing credits include: *Hour of the Wolf* (Malthouse, 2023), *Nosferatu* (Malthouse, 2023), *Poona* (Next Wave, 2021), *Control* (Red Stitch Actors Theatre, 2019), *Help Yourself* (MTC's Cybec Electric, 2019), *Luna* (VCA, 2019), and *Her Father's Daughter* (Hotel Now, 2018). *Nosferatu* and *Control* are published by Currency Press.

ISABELLA VADIVELOO
DIRECTOR

Isabella is a Naarm/Melbourne based theatre maker who works across disciplines as a theatre director, devisor and intimacy director. She has a strong interest in the development of new, form pushing and politically engaged performance. With both settler Australian and Tamil Sri Lankan heritage, Isabella prioritises centring underrepresented stories, often working with physical and body focused practices. Previous for Red Stitch, Isabella has directed *Wolf Play*. Other recent work includes *Atlantis* (Malthouse Theatre), *If Needed, Repeat* and *Unsuckle* (La Mama Theatre), *Poona* (Next Wave Festival), *Cybec Electric* and *First Stage* (Melbourne Theatre Company). She was Assistant Director for Melbourne Theatre

Company's production of *Sexual Misconduct* of the Middle Classes. Isabella has worked with The Dig Collective, Teatro De Los Sentidos, as well as presenting works for the Melbourne Fringe, Crack Theatre, Immerse and Village Festivals.

BIANCA PARDO
SET AND COSTUME DESIGN

Bianca is a passionate Melbourne/Naarm-based designer and maker. Both set and costume excite her and she endeavours to create visceral storytelling experiences through her craft. Bianca graduated from the Victorian College of the Arts (VCA) with a Bachelor of Fine Arts (Production - Design Realisation) in 2019. Bianca's design credits include *En Masse* (Rawcus), *One Day in September* (Perryman Theatre Company), *Suessical* (OCPAC), *Guys and Dolls, Passing Strange* (Antipodes Theatre Company), *TakeBack!* (Multicultural Arts Victoria), *Ngarngk: Giver of Life* (La Mama/YIRRAMBOI Festival); *Fucking A, Mad Forest* (VCA), *L'Oréal For Women in Science and Kenworth's Legacy* (Moo Motion), Associate Designer on *Mother Play*, Assistant Designer on *A Streetcar Named Desire* (Melbourne Theatre Company) and Costume Assistant on *Interior* (Rawcus). Bianca was awarded the Orloff Family Charitable Trust Scholarship in 2018 and was nominated for two Green Room Awards for her *Guys and Dolls* design. Throughout 2024, Bianca completed the Besen Family Artist Program at the Malthouse Theatre with placements on *The Hate Race* and *Fuck Christmas*. She is thrilled to be continuing in the Future Creatives Program at Melbourne Theatre Company this year.

RACHEL LEE
LIGHTING DESIGN

Rachel is a lighting designer and artist based in Naarm. She works primarily with new writing and is the co-creator of theatre collective MASHH (Mm And

Something Happens Here). Rachel designs across several companies and festivals including *Never Have I Ever, Topdog/Underdog, Never Have I Ever, I Wanna Be Yours , Laurinda* and *The Heartbreak Choir* (Melbourne Theatre Company), *Manifesto* and *Escalator* (Stephanie Lake Company), *Death of A Salesman* (GWB Entertainment and Red Line), *The Hate Race, Telethon Kid, Stay Woke* and *Hello, World!* (Malthouse Theatre), *Gender Euphoria* (Mama Alto and Maude Davey), *Peacemongers* and *Security* (Darebin Speakeasy), *Single Ladies* and *Ulster American* (Red Stitch Actors' Theatre), *Easy Riders* (APHIDS) and various installation works across Flash Forward (City of Melbourne). She has been nominated and awarded several Green Room Awards. MASHH is an award-winning collective that has been creating and presenting works since 2017. Recent works include *I Am Seaweed* and 《落叶 归根》 *(Luò yè guī gēn) Getting* (Singapore M1 Fringe Festival & Melbourne Fringe Festival).

GRACE FERGUSON
COMPOSITION/SOUND DESIGN

Grace Ferguson is an artist and teacher based in Naarm/Melbourne. Since studying piano performance at the MCM, she has been an active member of the arts community, producing original music, performing live and collaborating with others across the forms of theatre, dance and film. Her contemporary works draw from encounters, ranging from the ordinary to the mythic and primarily explore the undercurrents that exist within and around us. Informed by historic traditions, harmonic textures weave moments of gentle propulsion, robust outcry and fleeting nuance to give voice to individual and collective states of mind. Often combining composed and improvised material, she continually examines the tension between the planned and practiced, and what remains out of our control. Grace is represented as an Associate Artist by the Australian Music Centre. In 2024, she was awarded Best Original Score for a Main Stage Production for the production *On the Beach* (STC) at the Sydney Theatre Awards, shortlisted as a finalist for the APRA PD Awards (Classical/Experimental) and through the support of Creative Australia spent three months developing her practice as a resident at La Cité internationale des arts in France.

ETHAN HUNTER
COMPOSITION/SOUND DESIGN

Ethan Hunter (he/him) is a sound designer and VCA graduate (BFA Design & Production) working across theatre, dance, film, and installation. His recent notable credits include sound design for *Who's Afraid of Virginia Woolf?* (2023, 2024) with Red Stitch Actors' Theatre & GWB Productions, *Boys on the Verge of Tears* (2025) at fortyfivedownstairs, *Laundry Shoot* (2024), *MinusOneSister* (2023) at Theatre Works, and several graduate productions at VCA, such as *Plant Nation* (2024), *Theatrum Botanicum* (2022), and *The Wolves* (2022). Ethan has also collaborated with Masters of Theatre (Directing) students on captivating projects like *Ariadne* (2021), and *An Unseasonable Fall of Snow* (2022) at VCA. Ethan has completed secondments with Malthouse and Melbourne Theatre Company, contributing to productions like, *Macbeth (an Undoing)*, *Laurinda* and *Cyrano*. In addition, Ethan has worked as a Sound Engineer at companies such as Malthouse and Melbourne Theatre Company as well as touring with Chunky Move's *4/4* and *U>N>I>T>E>D*.

JESSICA SMART
STAGE MANAGER

Jessica Smart is a Melbourne-based stage manager and a Victorian College of the Arts (VCA) graduate with a Bachelor of Fine Arts (Production). Her recent Stage Manager credits include *The Comeuppance* (Red Stitch), *POTUS; Or Behind Every Great Dumbass Are Seven Women Trying To Keep Him Alive* (Lightning

Jar Theatre & fortyfivedownstairs), *Blacknificense: The Cotton Club Experience* (Midsumma Festival), *Zaffé* (Arts House), *Milked* (Ninth Floor Productions), and *Hamlet* (Melbourne Shakespeare Company). Her VCA credits include Assistant Stage Manager on *Urinetown: the Musical*, Stage Manager on *INCONSOLABLE Plus 4*, and Assistant Production Manager on *Heathers: The Musical*, in addition to completing internships on *Is God Is* (Melbourne Theatre Company) and *Telethon Kid* (Malthouse Theatre).

ELLA THOMPSON
ASSISTANT STAGE MANAGER

Ella Thompson is a stage manager who is new to the Naarm theatre scene. After completing a bachelor in performing arts majoring in stage management at WAAPA, Ella moved to Melbourne to continue her passion for the arts. Recently she was a technical stage manager for the Melbourne International Comedy Festival, Stage Manager/Operator and props for Soldier Boy (Theatreworks) and she is currently a producer for Tayo Tayo Collective. She is so excited to be working on her first production with Red Stitch!

KEVIN HOFBAUER
SIMON

Kevin Hofbauer has been consistently working in both theatre and film since he graduated from the Victorian College of the Arts in 2009. His start began on the hit television drama *Rush* as he was cast as season regular "Christian Tapu". He has been a Red Stitch ensemble member since 2014 after being cast as Avery in *The Flick* by Annie Baker, which was remounted twice, including a tour to Queensland. Red Stitch credits include: *The Flick, Trevor, The Way Out, Fast Food, Wolf Play* and *A Case for the Existence of God, The Comeuppance.* Other theatre credits include: *Atlantis* (Malthouse Theatre), *Macbeth* (MTC), *Touching the Void* (MTC), *Hour of the Wolf* (Malthouse Theatre)

Television credits include: *Rush, Small Time Gangster, Mr & Mrs Murder, Offspring, Sisters, True Story with Hamish and Andy, Playing for Keeps, Informer 3838, Neighbours, Clickbait, Spreadsheet* and *Planet Lulin*.

CARISSA LEE
LIA

Carissa Lee is a Noongar actor born on Wemba Wemba Country. She has performed with Melbourne Theatre Company, the Malthouse, Ilbijerri Theatre, and State Theatre Company of South Australia. Her most recent theatre credits include Maurial Spearim's comedy *Inside Out* with Yirramboi Festival, and Nazaree Dickerson's Noongar family play *Ngarngk*. Onscreen, Carissa has appeared in ABC's *Planet Lulin* and *Sammy J*, miniseries *Behind the Seams*, and horror film *The Dysphoria*. Since obtaining her PhD through the University of Melbourne, she also works as a cultural safety researcher, dramaturg and editor in her fellowship with Swinburne University of Technology.

CHRISTINA O'NEILL
JO

Christina graduated from WAAPA in 2005 and has since carved out a successful stage and screen career. Most recently she appeared in *Bloom* (Sydney Theatre Company) and *My Brilliant Career* (Melbourne Theatre Company). Her previous Red Stitch Actors' Theatre credits as an Ensemble member include: *Control, Right Now, The River, Middletown, Belleville, Straight, The Motherf*cker with the Hat*. Her other theatre credits include: *Hour of the Wolf* (Malthouse Theatre); *Girl from the North Country* (GWB Entertainment); *Calamity Jane* (One Eyed Man Productions); *Well, That Happened* (Melbourne Theatre Company); *Vivid White* (Melbourne Theatre Company); *Show Boat* (The Production Company); *Into the Woods, Sunday in the Park with George* (Victorian Opera); *Avenue Q* (Arts

Asia Pacific); *Spamalot* (Louise Withers and Associates); *Priscilla, Queen of the Desert: The Musical* (Back Row Productions). Television includes: *Neighbours, The Power of the Dream, Mr Black, Winners & Losers, City Homicide.* Albums: *Priscilla Queen of the Desert, Showqueen.* Awards: Helpmann, Best Supporting Actress in a Musical (*Avenue Q*).

ROISIN WALLACE NASH
HANSEN GRADUATE ASSISTANT DIRECTOR

Roisin Wallace Nash is an Irish-Australian performer, director, Theatre-maker and recent graduate of the Western Australian Academy of Performing Arts with a Bachelor of Performance Making. Over the past five years, she has worked and trained extensively with notable companies such as Queensland Theatre, Zen Zen Zo, LA MAMA Theatre, Brink Productions and The Blue Room Theatre. Roisin has received the Brisbane Immersive Ensemble Award for Outstanding Production for *SHELTER* and became the 2024 recipient of the Order of Australia Association Foundation Scholarship for Performing Arts.

SOOKYUNG SHIN
HANSEN GRADUATE ATTACHMENT

Sookyung is an actor from South Korea and a recent graduate of the Western Australia Academy of Performing Arts, where she completed a Bachelor of Acting. She has performed on stage as Nora 2 in *A Doll's House* (directed by Sonya Suares, adapted by Stef Smith), Dina Massie in *Beautiful Burnout* (directed by Matt Edgerton, by Frantic Assembly), and Miss Sheily in *The Harp in the South* (directed by Andrew Lewis, based on Ruth Park's novel). Sookyung is driven by the belief that acting has the power to offer a meaningful impact on others. This impact can sometimes bring moments of realization or, at other times, provide comfort, leaving a lasting influence on people. Her passion for acting stems from this very desire—to connect, inspire, and create powerful experiences that resonate deeply with her audience.

RED STITCH ACTORS' THEATRE

Red Stitch is a creative hub, offering scope for artists to make work they are passionate about in a sector where such opportunities are limited. As the ensemble and executives of Red Stitch, we provide a platform where leading practitioners can hone their craft and take risks, and emerging artists can work alongside mid-career and seasoned professionals. We play a vital role in the development and presentation of new Australian works through our INK playwriting program, promoting local voices alongside acclaimed contemporary international work which may not otherwise be seen by local audiences.

www.redstitch.net

Red Stitch would like to thank the following supporters who generously contribute to our INK program.

CΦPYRIGHTAGENCY
CULTURAL FUND

CREATIVE VICTORIA

Cybec
Foundation

MALCOLM ROBERTSON FOUNDATION

THE ROBERT SALZER FOUNDATION

S.B.W
Foundation

SEABORN, BROUGHTON &
WALFORD FOUNDATION
Supporting the Performing Arts

PLAYKING
FOUNDATION

Lyngala
Foundation

HANSEN LITTLE
FOUNDATION

SIDNEY MYER FUND

Kindred

THE MYER
FOUNDATION

.

www.ingramcontent.com/pod-product-compliance
Lightning Source LLC
Chambersburg PA
CBHW050022090426
42734CB00021B/3378